From Aspiring to Inspiring: A Guide for New Managers on the Rise

Gerard Assey

From Aspiring to Inspiring:
A Guide for New Managers on the Rise

By

Gerard Assey

Published by:

Gerard Assey

19/18, Palli Arasan Street

Anna Nagar East

Chennai - 600 102

ISBN: 978-93-92492-76-1

(Image courtesy jcomp on Freepik: 'https://www.freepik.com' Thank You)

Table of Contents

Preface

Congratulations! Whether you have recently been promoted to a managerial role or aspire to become one, this small yet powerful book: **'From Aspiring to Inspiring: A Guide for New Managers on the Rise'** is designed to be your trusted companion on this journey to managerial excellence. Being a manager brings new challenges, responsibilities, and opportunities for growth. It requires a unique set of skills and attributes to lead and inspire a team, make strategic decisions, and drive results.

As you embark on this exciting phase of your career, it is crucial to equip yourself with the knowledge and tools necessary to thrive in your new role. This book is crafted with the purpose of providing you with practical insights, actionable strategies, and real-world examples to help you navigate the complexities of being a manager.

We understand the importance of building a strong foundation as a manager. From mastering leadership skills to fostering effective communication, from making sound decisions to driving change, this book covers a comprehensive range of topics essential for your success. Each chapter delves deep into a specific skill or attribute, providing in-depth understanding, benefits, and an action plan for development.

Drawing inspiration from renowned leaders and successful managers, we present you with practical examples from the corporate world that illustrate how these skills and attributes translate into real-life situations. These examples will inspire you, challenge you, and offer valuable lessons to apply in your own managerial journey.

We believe that continuous learning and personal growth are fundamental to success as a manager. With this in mind, we encourage you to embrace a growth mindset, seek opportunities for self-improvement, and actively apply the concepts discussed in this book. By doing so, you will enhance your abilities, build strong relationships, and make a positive impact on your team and organization.

Remember, becoming an exceptional manager is a continuous process. It requires dedication, perseverance, and a commitment to ongoing development. This book is not intended to provide all the answers, but rather to serve as a guide and catalyst for your personal and professional growth.

We invite you to dive into the chapters, reflect on the insights shared, and apply the practical strategies to your own managerial context. Embrace the challenges, seize the opportunities, and unleash your full potential as a manager.

Here's to your success as a newly promoted manager or an aspiring one!

Why Invest in Your Development?

Investing in your development before or at an early stage of assuming the role of a new manager offers several key benefits:

- ✓ Preparedness: Investing in your development early on allows you to be better prepared for the challenges and responsibilities of the managerial role. It helps you gain the necessary knowledge, skills, and mindset to excel in your new position.
- ✓ Confidence: Developing yourself as a manager instills confidence in your abilities. By investing in your development, you gain a deeper understanding of your role and acquire the necessary competencies to tackle challenges with confidence.
- ✓ Effective Leadership: Developing your skills early on enables you to become an effective leader from the start. It equips you with the tools to inspire and motivate your team, foster a positive work environment, and drive performance.
- ✓ Faster Adaptation: Investing in your development allows for a quicker adaptation to the demands of the managerial role. It helps you become familiar with best practices, industry trends, and effective management techniques, enabling you to navigate the role more seamlessly.
- ✓ Stronger Relationships: Developing your interpersonal skills early on as a manager helps build strong relationships with your team members, peers, and superiors. It promotes

open communication, trust, and collaboration, leading to a more productive and harmonious work environment.

- ✓ Long-Term Growth: Investing in your development at an early stage sets the foundation for long-term growth and advancement in your career. It positions you as a continuous learner and demonstrates your commitment to personal and professional growth.
- ✓ Enhanced Job Satisfaction: Developing yourself as a manager contributes to higher job satisfaction. As you gain competence in your role, overcome challenges, and achieve success, you are more likely to feel fulfilled and motivated in your work.
- ✓ Increased Opportunities: By investing in your development early on, you open yourself up to a wider range of opportunities. As your skills and expertise grow, you become eligible for higher-level roles, increased responsibilities, and new challenges within your organization or industry.
- ✓ Value to the Organization: Developing yourself as a manager adds value to your organization. It equips you to make informed decisions, lead effectively, and contribute to the organization's goals and success. Your growth as a manager benefits not only yourself but also the entire team and organization.
- ✓ Personal Fulfillment: Ultimately, investing in your development as a new manager brings personal fulfillment. It allows you to reach your full potential, make a meaningful impact, and

continuously grow both personally and professionally.

By investing in your development early on as a new manager, you position yourself for long-term success, personal fulfillment, and the ability to lead with confidence and competence. It is an investment that pays dividends not only in your immediate role but also throughout your career journey.

The Consequences and Repercussions of not Investing in Your Development

Not investing in your development before assuming a new managerial role can have various repercussions and consequences that can impact you, your subordinates, your superiors, and the organization as a whole:

- ✓ Lack of Preparedness: Without investing in your development, you may lack the necessary skills, knowledge, and confidence to effectively carry out your managerial responsibilities. This can lead to a steep learning curve, increased stress, and potential mistakes or missteps in your role.
- ✓ Suboptimal Performance: Insufficient development can result in suboptimal performance as a manager. You may struggle to meet expectations, make informed decisions, and effectively lead your team, leading to decreased productivity and potential disengagement among your subordinates.
- ✓ Strained Relationships: Your subordinates may feel unsupported and frustrated if you are ill-equipped to provide the guidance and support they need. This can lead to strained relationships, decreased morale, and a decline in trust and collaboration within the team.
- ✓ Missed Opportunities: Lack of development can limit your ability to identify and seize opportunities for growth and improvement.

You may miss out on advancements, promotions, and new challenges within the organization, which can hinder your long-term career prospects.

- ✓ Decreased Credibility: Insufficient development may lead to a lack of credibility in the eyes of your superiors, peers, and subordinates. Your ability to influence, persuade, and gain buy-in may be compromised, affecting your effectiveness as a leader.
- ✓ Stagnation: Failing to invest in your development can result in professional stagnation. You may become stuck in a comfort zone, relying on outdated practices and ideas, and missing out on personal and professional growth opportunities.
- ✓ Organizational Impact: A manager who has not invested in their development may struggle to align their actions and decisions with the organization's goals and strategies. This can have a ripple effect on team performance, overall productivity, and the achievement of organizational objectives.
- ✓ Talent Retention: The lack of investment in your development as a manager can impact talent retention within the organization. Subordinates may feel disillusioned, unfulfilled, or unchallenged under your leadership, leading to increased turnover and difficulty in attracting and retaining top talent.
- ✓ Missed Innovation: Without investing in your development, you may miss opportunities to stay updated with industry trends, new technologies, and innovative practices. This

can hinder your ability to drive innovation within your team and organization.

- ✓ Personal and Professional Frustration: Ultimately, the consequences of not investing in your development can lead to personal and professional frustration. You may feel stuck in your role, dissatisfied with your performance, and limited in your ability to achieve your full potential.

It is important to recognize that investing in your development as a manager is not only beneficial for your own growth but also crucial for the success of your team and the organization as a whole. By neglecting your development, you risk hindering your effectiveness as a leader, damaging relationships, and missing out on valuable opportunities for growth and advancement.

Doing a Pre- Self-Assessment to Know Where You Stand

Performing a self-assessment to evaluate your proficiency in various attributes requires a structured approach. Here are steps you can follow:

1. Identify the attributes: Begin by listing the attributes or skills you want to assess. Based on the skills and attributes we discussed earlier, create a comprehensive list that includes leadership, communication, decision-making, problem-solving, adaptability, emotional intelligence, time management, team building, strategic thinking, continuous learning, delegation, conflict resolution, coaching and mentoring, financial acumen, and influence and persuasion.
2. Set criteria: Define the criteria or indicators that will help you evaluate your proficiency in each attribute. These criteria can vary depending on the specific attribute. For example, for leadership, you may consider indicators like ability to inspire and motivate others, setting a clear vision, and empowering team members.
3. Rate yourself: Assign a rating scale (e.g., 1 to 5 or poor to excellent) to each criterion to assess your current level of proficiency. Be honest and objective in your self-evaluation. Consider your past experiences, feedback from others, and your own observations.
4. Gather evidence: Collect evidence or examples that support your self-assessment for each attribute. This evidence can come

from previous projects, feedback from colleagues or superiors, and personal achievements. It helps to have concrete examples to validate your self-assessment and provide context.

5. Reflect and analyze: Take time to reflect on your ratings and evidence. Analyze your strengths and areas for improvement in each attribute. Consider how these attributes align with your current or desired managerial role. Reflecting on your self-assessment helps you gain a deeper understanding of your skills and areas that need development.
6. Set goals: Based on your self-assessment, identify specific goals for each attribute. These goals should be actionable and measurable. For example, if you rated your delegation skills lower than desired, your goal could be "Delegate at least three tasks per week to team members and track their progress."
7. Create an action plan: Develop an action plan to improve your skills in the areas identified as weaknesses. Determine the steps you need to take, such as attending relevant training programs, seeking mentorship, or practicing specific techniques. Break down your action plan into manageable tasks and set deadlines for completion.
8. Implement and review: Execute your action plan and regularly review your progress. Monitor your growth in each attribute, celebrate achievements, and make adjustments as necessary. Seek feedback from others to gain an external perspective on your development.

Remember, self-assessment is an ongoing process, and you can repeat these steps periodically to track your progress and adapt your goals and action plans accordingly.

Before You Begin Working on Your Skills, Why the Right Attitude and Mindset is Most Important!

Irrespective of whatever profession or business you are in, you will know that while every business requires C.A.S.H. to survive and succeed....Every Professional also needs something to succeed, which I believe is more valuable than the CASH that comes in. This is 'K.A.S.H.' because only when you have this KASH in you, you will be more successful in bringing in the CASH for you and/or the organization you represent, by ensuring and protecting the credibility and image of the organization.

So what is this KASH?

- ✓ **K**nowledge
- ✓ **A**ttitude
- ✓ **S**kills
- ✓ **H**abits

Knowledge is all about a Company's Products or Services that is offered, the Market and Industry/domain that they operate in, together with knowing of who are the other players or the competition that are in this industry. It also involves knowing where your organization stands against them-their strengths and areas that the competition has an advantage over, along with being thorough on the rates, polices and regulations in the industry and market.

How effectively are you able to transfer any knowledge you possess, to the customer/ others to enable them to deal or decide upon the next step or you as their service provider or vendor is a skill.

Now there are various types of skill sets that people possess-Some examples for skills are:

Interpersonal Skills
Problem Solving Skills
Selling Skills
Networking Skills
Time Management
Team Working
Presentation Skills
Effective Probing Skills
Ability to present thoughts
Effective Communication Skills
People Handing Skills/ Inter-personal Skills

Having just Knowledge and Skills alone is not enough. There are many people you probably know of, that have a great bank of knowledge along with the necessary skills, but yet have been total failures. Reason being they had a lousy attitude or very poor habits that killed a potential sale or the potential in them; that ultimately affected theirs and their organizations credibility

What you are seeing on the pie chart is the mental make-up of a Professional.

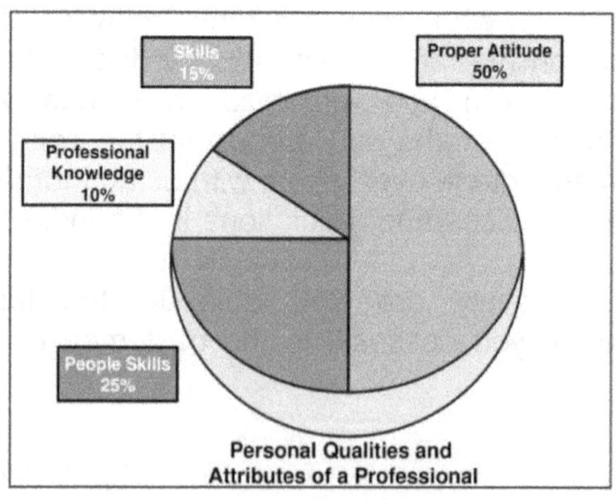

As you will see, 50% has to do with the Attitude, followed by 25% on People Skills. In other words, if you don't have the required knowledge or skills, as you can see, you may be able to still succeed with the right attitude and people skills, because those two account for 75%. Now don't get me wrong, I am not saying that you should not work on your knowledge and skills…Absolutely no!

What I am saying is that given that you have the right attitude coupled with the right people skills, knowledge and skills, you don't have to guess where your career graph would be!

Let us look at this a little differently….Assuming you have the right attitude and people skills, which together comprise of 75% but lack the required knowledge and skills, well then, to me, with the right attitude you can easily learn them. And one of the attributes that will pay dividends is someone who has a desire to learn or is teachable, as Knowledge and Skills are teachable, but not Attitude!

Attitude is the outlook or perception towards a given situation, and for any professional, this is extremely crucial and foundational-especially during a downtime! Attitude is made up from our upbringing, environment, exposure etc. It would therefore be very difficult or it would take a long time to undo a wrong attitude that has gone in all these years. And if you are working with other people, like that of sales, customer service or in other departments, then this is very important- as customers/ colleagues remember the wrong or negative attitude longer. You are the only thing the customer sometimes sees of your company- and this is the impression formed of your entire company- good or bad! It takes a long time to undo this negative feeling about your company in the mind of the customer.

At this stage it is important to realize that there are **3 A's of Business life**:

Ability, Ambition and **Attitude**

- ✓ Ability establishes 'what' someone does
- ✓ Ambition determines 'how much' he does
- ✓ But Attitude alone 'guarantees how' he does it!

Ability will bring one a pay cheque (check)

Ambition will get him a raise

Attitude alone will lead to success in everything!

Attitude is actually the 'YOU on the job. When ability and ambition in two people are about equal, how does the boss select one over the other for promotion? Here is where Attitude is the deciding factor. Attitude reflects a little plus- that something extra is given willingly though not required.

If you look at the word A-T-T-I-T-U-D-E itself, is it a mere coincidence that "I" comes first and "U" later? If this has any significance, then in trying to understand the attitudes of people, we should first examine ourselves in relation to other people!

Because Attitude is so very important, this is why it is so crucial to fill our minds with the right positive thoughts (especially when all the world seems flooded with negativity) because our thoughts work into decisions that form our actions and this continued action leads to a habit, which eventually makes up our attitude. Your habits today will become your attitude in the days to come. That's why it is important to check our habits as well. As an example: The habit of being late (at say your office), if not nipped in the early stages can lead it to becoming an attitude, with everything that you undertake being late or delayed!

Here are some examples of positive or right attitude:
Belief
Commitment
Ability to fail & learn from it
Persistent goals
Self-Motivation
Enthusiasm
Purpose
Self-discipline
Confidence
Creativity
Empathy
Go the extra mile
Self-improvement
Time organization...and most of all the *PASSION!*

Top Champions...

- ✓ Understand themselves and how their behavior affects others
- ✓ Have a positive attitude, which reflects in dedication to getting it right the first time, and commitment to helping others
- ✓ Know how to adapt their behavior to meet the differing needs of the situation
- ✓ A willingness to take responsibility
- ✓ Have the confidence to stay calm under pressure

Attitude Impacts Outcome

Steps to change your Attitude...

- ✓ Become aware of your negative attitude towards yourself, other people and situations and alter your thinking
- ✓ Think for yourself and become more constructive
- ✓ Keep an open mind

Remember: Changes are always: M.A.D.E...!!!

Developing GREAT Positive Attitudes is not something that happens to you-it is something you make happen…and like any change, it is not easy!
Here are some steps that can help:
M- Mental Pictures: Visualize who you are, what you want, how will you conduct and carry yourself. Formulate and stamp indelibly on your mind a mental picture of yourself as succeeding. Hold this picture tenaciously. Never permit it to fade. Your mind will seek to bring this picture into form.
A- Affirmations: Add a new self-image by talking positively
D- Daily Successes: Build confidence everyday by looking at your positives rather than negatives. Make a true estimate of your own ability, and then raise it 10 percent. Do not become egotistical but develop a wholesome self-respect.
E- Environmental Influences: Do not try to copy or be someone else. Nobody can be you as well as you can. But surround yourself with positive influencers, read positive stuff, listen and watch positive information etc
You are what you think! To change any habits, you must first change any thoughts, feelings and values!
Changing Bad Habits into Good Ones!
Step 1: List your bad habits
Step 2: What were the original causes?
Step 3: What are the supporting causes?
Step 4: Determine a positive habit to replace the bad one.
Step 5: Think about the good habit, its benefits and results.
Step 6: Take action to develop this habit.
Step 7: Daily act upon this habit for reinforcement.

Step 8: Reward yourself by noting one of the benefits from your good habit

You Begin Your Exciting Journey of Each Skill

Welcome to the journey of developing your most essential skills for managerial success! As you navigate the skills from now on, you will embark on a transformative exploration of key skills and attributes that are vital for your growth as a manager. Each skill we delve into holds the power to unlock your potential, enhance your effectiveness, and make a lasting impact on your team and organization.

By investing time and effort into developing these skills, you are taking a proactive step towards becoming a well-rounded and influential leader. The chapters ahead will equip you with practical insights, actionable strategies, and real-world examples to guide you on your path to mastery.

Remember, developing these skills is not an overnight process. It requires dedication, practice, and a commitment to continuous learning. As you embark on this journey, embrace the challenges, embrace the opportunities, and embrace your potential for growth.

Now, let us dive into the first skill, and move forward as we make progress. Explore the in-depth understanding, benefits, and action plan to enhance each skill, and discover how it can shape your managerial journey.

Are you ready to unlock your full potential?

Let's begin our exploration of the skills that will set you apart as an exceptional manager.

Leadership

Leadership is a critical skill for managers as it involves guiding and influencing others towards the achievement of shared goals. Here is an in-depth understanding of leadership, its benefits, importance, and an action plan to develop this skill as a new manager, along with specific examples from the corporate world.

Understanding Leadership: Leadership is the ability to inspire and motivate individuals or teams to achieve desired outcomes. It goes beyond a positional authority and encompasses qualities like effective communication, vision-setting, guidance, and empowerment. A strong leader fosters a positive work environment, promotes collaboration, and cultivates a sense of purpose among team members.

Benefits and Importance of Leadership:

- ✓ Enhanced Team Performance: Effective leadership inspires individuals to give their best effort, resulting in improved team performance and productivity. A skilled leader understands each team member's strengths, assigns tasks accordingly, and ensures the team is aligned with organizational goals.
- ✓ Employee Engagement and Retention: Leadership plays a significant role in employee engagement and retention. When employees feel valued, supported, and inspired by their leader, they are more likely to be engaged, satisfied, and committed to the organization.
- ✓ Effective Communication: Leaders with strong communication skills foster an open and

transparent work environment. They can convey information clearly, actively listen to their team members, provide feedback, and address concerns effectively. This enables better collaboration, understanding, and alignment within the team.

- ✓ Building Trust and Loyalty: Trust is essential in any successful team. A leader who demonstrates integrity, consistency, and reliability earns the trust and loyalty of their team members. Trust fosters strong relationships, encourages open dialogue, and leads to a higher level of commitment and collaboration.
- ✓ Succession Planning and Talent Development: Effective leaders understand the importance of talent development and succession planning. They identify and nurture potential leaders within their teams, providing mentorship, growth opportunities, and challenges that help individuals develop their skills and prepare for future leadership roles.

Action Plan to Develop Leadership Skills:

- ✓ Set a Clear Vision: Define your team's vision and communicate it clearly to your members. A compelling vision inspires and guides the team towards shared goals. Develop a vision statement that encapsulates the team's purpose, values, and long-term objectives.
- ✓ Practice Effective Communication: Enhance your communication skills by actively listening, providing feedback, and expressing ideas clearly. Foster open communication channels, hold regular team meetings, and encourage

two-way dialogue to ensure everyone feels heard and understood.

- ✓ Lead by Example: Exhibit the behaviors and qualities you expect from your team. Demonstrate integrity, professionalism, and a strong work ethic. Be approachable, empathetic, and supportive, building a positive work culture.
- ✓ Empower and Delegate: Delegate tasks to team members based on their strengths and provide them with autonomy and responsibility. Trust their abilities, offer guidance and resources, and recognize their achievements. Empowered employees become more engaged and take ownership of their work.
- ✓ Seek Professional Development: Invest in your own leadership development through workshops, courses, or mentoring programs. Stay updated with industry trends, leadership best practices, and new strategies. Continuous learning helps you refine your leadership skills and stay ahead.

Examples from the Corporate World:

- ✓ Satya Nadella (Microsoft): Satya Nadella, as the CEO of Microsoft, transformed the company's culture by focusing on empathy, collaboration, and a growth mindset. His leadership approach fostered innovation and motivated employees to embrace change and drive the company's success.
- ✓ Mary Barra (General Motors): Mary Barra, the CEO of General Motors, prioritized transparency and accountability to rebuild trust within the organization. Her leadership

style emphasized open communication, encouraging employees to voice their opinions and contribute to the company's growth.

- ✓ Indra Nooyi (Former CEO of PepsiCo): Indra Nooyi, during her tenure as CEO of PepsiCo, emphasized the importance of purpose-driven leadership. She set ambitious sustainability goals, prioritized employee well-being, and promoted diversity and inclusion, creating a strong sense of purpose and commitment within the organization.
- ✓ By following this action plan and drawing inspiration from successful leaders, you can develop and enhance your leadership skills as a new manager. Remember, leadership is an ongoing journey, and continuous improvement and adaptation are crucial for long-term success.

Communication

Understanding Communication: Communication is the process of exchanging information, ideas, and emotions between individuals or groups. It involves both verbal and non-verbal cues, active listening, and the ability to convey messages clearly and effectively. As a manager, your communication skills impact your ability to provide direction, build relationships, motivate your team, and resolve conflicts.

Benefits and Importance of Communication:

- ✓ Clarity and Understanding: Effective communication ensures that messages are conveyed clearly, leaving no room for confusion or misinterpretation. It helps align everyone's understanding of goals, expectations, and tasks, leading to increased productivity and efficiency.
- ✓ Collaboration and Teamwork: Strong communication skills foster collaboration within teams. Managers who communicate openly and transparently create an environment where team members feel comfortable sharing ideas, seeking feedback, and working together towards common objectives.
- ✓ Conflict Resolution: Effective communication is crucial in resolving conflicts. It allows managers to listen to different perspectives, address concerns, and find mutually beneficial solutions. Clear and empathetic communication helps build trust, reduce

tensions, and maintain positive working relationships.

- ✓ Motivation and Engagement: When managers communicate effectively, they inspire and motivate their team members. By sharing the organization's vision, acknowledging individual contributions, and providing regular feedback, managers boost employee morale and engagement.
- ✓ Building Relationships: Communication is the foundation of strong relationships. Managers who actively listen, show empathy, and communicate honestly build trust and rapport with their team members. Positive relationships foster loyalty, open dialogue, and a supportive work environment.

Action Plan to Develop Communication Skills:

- ✓ Active Listening: Practice active listening by giving your full attention to others during conversations. Avoid interrupting, ask clarifying questions, and demonstrate empathy. Make a conscious effort to understand not just the words being spoken but also the underlying emotions and perspectives.
- ✓ Clarity and Conciseness: Strive for clear and concise communication. Use simple language, organize your thoughts beforehand, and avoid jargon or technical terms that might confuse others. Tailor your communication style to suit the needs and preferences of your team members.
- ✓ Non-Verbal Communication: Pay attention to your non-verbal cues, such as body language, facial expressions, and tone of voice. Ensure

that your non-verbal signals align with your verbal messages. Practice conveying confidence, approachability, and openness through your non-verbal communication.

- ✓ Feedback and Recognition: Develop the habit of providing timely and constructive feedback to your team members. Be specific, focusing on behavior and outcomes, and offer suggestions for improvement. Similarly, acknowledge and recognize achievements to motivate and reinforce positive performance.
- ✓ Conflict Resolution: Learn conflict resolution techniques such as active listening, paraphrasing, and finding common ground. Practice remaining calm and composed during conflicts, encouraging open dialogue, and mediating disputes to find mutually agreeable solutions.

Examples from the Corporate World:

- ✓ Sheryl Sandberg (Facebook): Sheryl Sandberg, as the COO of Facebook, is known for her excellent communication skills. She encourages open and transparent communication within the company and emphasizes the importance of feedback and effective team collaboration.
- ✓ Tim Cook (Apple): Tim Cook, as the CEO of Apple, is known for his clear and concise communication style. His messages to employees and stakeholders are often straightforward, ensuring that his vision and expectations are understood by all.
- ✓ Mary Barra (General Motors): Mary Barra, the CEO of General Motors, emphasizes open and honest communication throughout the

organization. She encourages employees to voice their opinions, actively listens to their concerns, and fosters a culture of open dialogue.

By following this action plan and drawing inspiration from successful leaders, you can develop and enhance your communication skills as a new manager. Remember to practice consistently, seek feedback, and adapt your communication style to suit different situations and individuals.

Decision-making

Understanding Decision-Making: Decision-making is the process of selecting the best course of action among various alternatives. Managers often face complex and ambiguous situations that require them to make informed choices. Effective decision-making involves gathering relevant information, analyzing options, considering potential risks and outcomes, and making timely decisions.

Benefits and Importance of Decision-Making:

- ✓ Problem Solving: Decision-making and problem-solving go hand in hand. By making effective decisions, managers address challenges and solve problems in a systematic and logical manner. This leads to more efficient processes, improved outcomes, and increased productivity.
- ✓ Resource Allocation: Managers are responsible for allocating resources such as budgets, personnel, and time. Sound decision-making helps managers allocate resources effectively and optimize their utilization, resulting in cost savings, improved efficiency, and better overall performance.
- ✓ Risk Management: Decision-making involves assessing potential risks and weighing them against potential rewards. Managers who make informed decisions are better equipped to identify and mitigate risks, reducing the likelihood of negative consequences and enhancing the organization's resilience.
- ✓ Adaptability and Innovation: Effective decision-making enables managers to

respond to changes in the business environment and drive innovation. By analyzing information and considering alternative options, managers can identify new opportunities, initiate changes, and foster a culture of continuous improvement.

- ✓ Employee Engagement: When managers make decisions in a transparent and inclusive manner, it fosters a sense of ownership and engagement among team members. Involving employees in the decision-making process can increase their motivation, job satisfaction, and commitment to organizational goals.

Action Plan to Develop Decision-Making Skills:

- ✓ Gather Relevant Information: When faced with a decision, start by gathering all relevant information. Identify the key factors, data, and perspectives that are necessary to make an informed choice. Utilize various sources, such as research, reports, and input from subject matter experts.
- ✓ Analyze Options: Evaluate different alternatives and their potential outcomes. Consider the pros and cons of each option, and assess their alignment with organizational goals and values. Use analytical tools, such as SWOT analysis or decision matrices, to objectively evaluate the options.
- ✓ Consider Risks and Consequences: Identify potential risks and assess their impact on the decision-making process. Consider both short-term and long-term consequences of each alternative. Develop contingency plans or mitigation strategies to address potential risks.

- ✓ Seek Input and Collaboration: Involve relevant stakeholders and team members in the decision-making process. Seek diverse perspectives and encourage open dialogue. Collaboration can lead to better decisions by leveraging the collective knowledge and expertise of the team.
- ✓ Make Timely Decisions: Avoid unnecessary delays and analysis paralysis. Set a timeline for decision-making and adhere to it. Consider the urgency of the situation and the potential impact of delaying the decision. Communicate decisions clearly and provide the necessary guidance for implementation.

Examples from the Corporate World:

- ✓ Jeff Bezos (Amazon): Jeff Bezos, the founder and former CEO of Amazon, is known for his emphasis on data-driven decision-making. Amazon's success can be attributed, in part, to its commitment to gathering and analyzing vast amounts of data to make informed choices regarding customer experience, product development, and business strategies.
- ✓ Mary Barra (General Motors): Mary Barra, the CEO of General Motors, made a crucial decision to focus on electric vehicles and shift the company's strategic direction. This decision reflected the changing market trends and the need for sustainable mobility solutions, positioning General Motors as a leader in the industry.
- ✓ Satya Nadella (Microsoft): Satya Nadella, as the CEO of Microsoft, made significant decisions to shift the company's focus towards

cloud computing and digital transformation. These decisions allowed Microsoft to adapt to changing market dynamics and regain its position as a technology industry leader.

By following this action plan and drawing inspiration from successful decision-makers, you can develop and enhance your decision-making skills as a new manager. Continuously evaluate the outcomes of your decisions, learn from them, and refine your approach over time. Remember, decision-making is a skill that can be honed through practice, experience, and a willingness to learn from both successes and failures.

Problem-solving

Understanding Problem-Solving: Problem-solving is the process of identifying, analyzing, and resolving challenges or obstacles that hinder the achievement of goals or desired outcomes. Managers encounter various problems in their roles, ranging from operational issues to strategic dilemmas. Effective problem-solving involves adopting a systematic approach, considering alternative solutions, thinking critically, and involving relevant stakeholders.

Benefits and Importance of Problem-Solving:

- ✓ Efficiency and Productivity: Effective problem-solving increases efficiency and productivity within an organization. Managers who tackle challenges head-on and develop optimal solutions minimize disruptions and bottlenecks, enabling smooth operations.
- ✓ Innovation and Growth: Problem-solving often leads to innovation and growth opportunities. By identifying and addressing problems, managers can uncover new ways of doing things, improve processes, and create a culture of continuous improvement and innovation.
- ✓ Decision-Making: Problem-solving and decision-making are closely intertwined. Managers who can effectively solve problems gather relevant information, analyze options, and make informed decisions. Strong problem-solving skills enhance the quality and effectiveness of decision-making.
- ✓ Team Collaboration: Problem-solving often requires collaboration and input from various

stakeholders. Managers who involve their team members in the problem-solving process foster a sense of ownership, engagement, and teamwork. Collaboration brings diverse perspectives and expertise to find the best solutions.

- ✓ Adaptability and Resilience: Problem-solving helps managers navigate uncertainties and changes. By developing problem-solving skills, managers become more adaptable, resilient, and capable of handling unexpected challenges, enabling them to steer their teams through dynamic environments.

Action Plan to Develop Problem-Solving Skills:

- ✓ Identify the Problem: Clearly define the problem by gathering information and understanding its root causes. Ask relevant questions and seek input from team members or stakeholders who may have insights into the problem.
- ✓ Analyze and Break Down the Problem: Break down the problem into manageable components. Identify patterns, dependencies, and potential impacts. Use tools like cause-and-effect diagrams, process mapping, or fishbone diagrams to analyze the problem systematically.
- ✓ Generate Alternative Solutions: Brainstorm and explore different options and potential solutions. Encourage creativity and open-mindedness. Evaluate the pros and cons of each alternative, considering feasibility, potential outcomes, and alignment with organizational goals.

- ✓ Think Critically: Apply critical thinking skills to evaluate the alternatives objectively. Consider the potential risks and consequences of each solution. Seek diverse perspectives and challenge assumptions to ensure comprehensive analysis.
- ✓ Select and Implement the Best Solution: Based on the evaluation, choose the most suitable solution. Develop an implementation plan, considering resources, timelines, and potential obstacles. Communicate the solution effectively to stakeholders and gain their support.
- ✓ Evaluate and Learn: Assess the effectiveness of the solution and monitor its implementation. Evaluate the outcomes and learn from the process. Identify lessons learned and areas for improvement to enhance future problem-solving capabilities.

Examples from the Corporate World:

- ✓ Elon Musk (Tesla, SpaceX): Elon Musk faced the challenge of building sustainable and affordable electric vehicles. Through innovative problem-solving, he implemented advanced battery technologies, developed charging infrastructure, and revolutionized the electric vehicle industry.
- ✓ Sundar Pichai (Google): Sundar Pichai led Google through the problem-solving process of diversifying its products beyond search. He fostered a culture of experimentation and exploration, resulting in the development of products like Google Chrome, Android, and Google Cloud.

- ✓ Mary Barra (General Motors): Mary Barra, as the CEO of General Motors, tackled the problem of product recalls and quality issues. She initiated a company-wide focus on quality, safety, and customer satisfaction, leading to significant improvements and restoring trust in the brand.

By following this action plan and drawing inspiration from successful problem-solvers, you can develop and enhance your problem-solving skills as a new manager. Remember to approach problems systematically, involve others, and learn from each problem-solving experience to continuously improve your capabilities.

Adaptability

Understanding Adaptability: Adaptability is the ability to adjust and thrive in a rapidly changing business environment. It involves cultivating a mindset of flexibility, open-mindedness, and willingness to learn. Adaptable managers embrace new technologies, ideas, and methodologies to stay ahead, guide their teams through change, and seize opportunities for growth.

Benefits and Importance of Adaptability:

- ✓ Resilience and Agility: Adaptable managers can quickly respond to unforeseen challenges and changes. They demonstrate resilience in the face of adversity and are capable of shifting strategies, reallocating resources, and finding innovative solutions to overcome obstacles.
- ✓ Future Readiness: The business landscape is constantly evolving due to technological advancements, market trends, and competitive forces. Adaptable managers stay ahead by proactively seeking opportunities, embracing emerging technologies, and keeping up with industry trends to ensure their teams remain competitive.
- ✓ Employee Engagement: Managers who demonstrate adaptability create an environment that encourages creativity, experimentation, and growth. This fosters a culture of continuous learning and improvement, leading to higher levels of employee engagement, job satisfaction, and retention.

- ✓ Change Management: In times of organizational change, adaptable managers play a crucial role in guiding their teams through transitions. Their ability to communicate effectively, manage resistance, and adapt processes ensures a smoother change implementation and minimizes disruptions.
- ✓ Innovation and Problem-Solving: Adaptability fosters a mindset that embraces new ideas and encourages experimentation. Adaptable managers are more likely to explore innovative solutions and think creatively, leading to improved problem-solving capabilities and fostering a culture of innovation within their teams.

Action Plan to Develop Adaptability:

- ✓ Embrace a Growth Mindset: Cultivate a mindset that views challenges and changes as opportunities for growth and learning. Adopt a positive attitude towards change, seek out new experiences, and be open to feedback and constructive criticism.
- ✓ Stay Informed: Keep yourself updated with industry trends, emerging technologies, and best practices. Regularly read industry publications, attend webinars or conferences, and participate in relevant professional development programs. Stay connected with industry networks to broaden your knowledge and insights.
- ✓ Foster a Learning Culture: Encourage a culture of continuous learning and growth within your team. Provide opportunities for skill development, offer cross-training initiatives,

and support employees in attending training programs or pursuing certifications.

- ✓ Encourage Experimentation: Create a safe environment where team members feel comfortable taking calculated risks and trying new approaches. Encourage creativity, reward innovative ideas, and provide support for experimentation.
- ✓ Lead by Example: Demonstrate adaptability in your own actions and decisions. Be willing to adapt strategies, change course when needed, and embrace new technologies or methodologies. Show your team that you are open to feedback and willing to learn from mistakes.

Examples from the Corporate World:

- ✓ Satya Nadella (Microsoft): Satya Nadella, as the CEO of Microsoft, led the company through a transformative phase by embracing cloud computing and shifting its focus to a subscription-based model. This adaptability allowed Microsoft to evolve and remain competitive in the rapidly changing technology industry.
- ✓ Reed Hastings (Netflix): Reed Hastings, the co-founder and CEO of Netflix, demonstrated adaptability by successfully transitioning the company from a DVD rental service to a leading streaming platform. He recognized the changing landscape of entertainment consumption and adapted the business model accordingly.
- ✓ Mary Barra (General Motors): Mary Barra, the CEO of General Motors, embraced adaptability by prioritizing electric and

autonomous vehicles to position the company for the future of mobility. Under her leadership, General Motors has invested heavily in new technologies and transformed its product lineup to meet evolving consumer demands.

By following this action plan and drawing inspiration from successful adaptable leaders, you can develop and enhance your adaptability as a new manager. Remember to be proactive, embrace change, foster a learning culture, and lead by example to navigate the evolving business landscape successfully.

Emotional Intelligence

Understanding Emotional Intelligence: Emotional intelligencc (EI) refers to the ability to recognize, understand, and manage emotions, both in oneself and others. As a manager, having a high level of EI is essential for building strong relationships, effectively communicating, and fostering a positive work environment. It involves self-awareness, empathy, and the ability to regulate emotions.

Benefits and Importance of Emotional Intelligence:

- ✓ Building Relationships: Emotional intelligence helps managers build strong and trusting relationships with their team members. By understanding others' emotions and perspectives, managers can communicate effectively, show empathy, and establish a supportive work environment.
- ✓ Conflict Resolution: EI plays a crucial role in resolving conflicts. Managers with high EI can effectively navigate and manage conflicts by understanding the emotions involved, actively listening to different perspectives, and finding solutions that meet the needs of all parties involved.
- ✓ Team Collaboration: Emotional intelligence promotes teamwork and collaboration. Managers who possess EI can effectively manage diverse personalities, encourage open communication, and leverage the strengths of each team member to foster a cohesive and high-performing team.

- ✓ Employee Engagement: Managers with high EI can better understand the emotions and needs of their team members. This understanding enables them to provide support, recognition, and opportunities for growth, resulting in increased employee engagement, satisfaction, and retention.
- ✓ Leadership Effectiveness: Emotional intelligence is a key attribute of effective leadership. Managers with high EI can inspire and motivate their team members, handle stressful situations, make informed decisions, and adapt their leadership style to different individuals and circumstances.

Action Plan to Develop Emotional Intelligence:

- ✓ Develop Self-Awareness: Reflect on your own emotions, triggers, and reactions. Pay attention to your strengths and areas for improvement. Engage in self-reflection exercises, keep a journal, or seek feedback from trusted colleagues to enhance your self-awareness.
- ✓ Practice Active Listening: Engage in active listening to understand others' perspectives and emotions. Pay attention to non-verbal cues, show genuine interest, and validate others' feelings. Practice empathetic listening to build stronger connections and foster trust.
- ✓ Cultivate Empathy: Put yourself in others' shoes and seek to understand their emotions and experiences. Develop empathy by actively listening, asking open-ended questions, and demonstrating understanding and compassion. Show genuine care for your team members' well-being.

- ✓ Manage Emotions: Learn to recognize and manage your own emotions in various situations. Practice techniques like deep breathing, mindfulness, or taking a pause before responding. Develop strategies to handle stress, frustrations, and conflicts in a constructive manner.
- ✓ Seek Feedback: Request feedback from your team members and colleagues on how you handle emotions and interpersonal interactions. Actively listen to their perspectives and use the feedback as an opportunity for growth and improvement.

Examples from the Corporate World:

- ✓ Satya Nadella (Microsoft): Satya Nadella, as the CEO of Microsoft, is known for his strong emotional intelligence. He promotes a culture of empathy and inclusion within the organization, actively listens to employees, and fosters a supportive work environment.
- ✓ Indra Nooyi (Former CEO of PepsiCo): Indra Nooyi displayed high emotional intelligence during her tenure as the CEO of PepsiCo. She prioritized employee well-being, encouraged open communication, and recognized the importance of understanding and addressing the emotions and needs of her team members.
- ✓ Daniel Goleman (Author and Psychologist): Daniel Goleman popularized the concept of emotional intelligence and its significance in leadership and organizational success. His work emphasizes the importance of self-awareness, empathy, and effective emotional management in the workplace.

By following this action plan and drawing inspiration from successful leaders, you can develop and enhance your emotional intelligence as a new manager. Remember to continuously practice self-awareness, empathy, and effective emotional management to build strong relationships, handle conflicts, and foster a positive work environment.

Time Management

Understanding Time Management: Time management refers to the ability to effectively allocate and utilize time to accomplish tasks and achieve goals. For managers who handle multiple responsibilities, mastering time management is crucial. It involves prioritizing tasks, setting goals, delegating when appropriate, and using strategies to maximize productivity and meet deadlines.

Benefits and Importance of Time Management:

- ✓ Increased Productivity: Effective time management helps managers accomplish more in less time. By setting priorities, organizing tasks, and avoiding time-wasting activities, managers can optimize their productivity and make the most of their working hours.
- ✓ Better Work-Life Balance: By managing time effectively, managers can strike a balance between work and personal life. Prioritizing and allocating time for personal activities, hobbies, and relaxation enhances well-being and reduces burnout, leading to increased job satisfaction and overall happiness.
- ✓ Meeting Deadlines: Time management ensures that managers meet deadlines consistently. By planning tasks and allocating sufficient time for each, managers can avoid last-minute rushes, reduce stress, and maintain a track record of delivering work on time.
- ✓ Stress Reduction: Effective time management reduces stress levels. By having a clear plan,

staying organized, and managing priorities, managers can minimize the feeling of being overwhelmed and maintain a sense of control over their workload.

- ✓ Improved Decision-Making: When managers manage their time well, they have more time for reflection and critical thinking. This allows for better decision-making, as managers can consider alternatives, gather information, and analyze situations more thoroughly.

Action Plan to Develop Time Management Skills:

- ✓ Set Clear Goals: Define your short-term and long-term goals as a manager. Break down these goals into specific tasks and milestones. Clear goals provide focus and direction, enabling you to prioritize your time effectively.
- ✓ Prioritize Tasks: Identify the most important and urgent tasks that align with your goals. Prioritize these tasks based on their impact and deadlines. Focus on high-priority activities to ensure that critical objectives are met.
- ✓ Plan and Organize: Create a daily, weekly, or monthly schedule to allocate time for specific tasks and activities. Use productivity tools such as calendars, to-do lists, or project management software to keep track of your tasks and deadlines. Organize your workspace to minimize distractions and create an environment conducive to productivity.
- ✓ Delegate and Empower: Recognize tasks that can be delegated to team members. Assess their skills and capabilities and assign appropriate responsibilities. Delegation not only helps distribute workload but also

develops team members' skills and fosters a sense of ownership.

- ✓ Avoid Time Wasters: Identify and minimize activities that consume time without adding value. Examples include excessive meetings, excessive time spent on emails, or distractions from social media. Set boundaries and establish time limits for these activities to maintain focus and productivity.

Examples from the Corporate World:

- ✓ Elon Musk (Tesla, SpaceX): Elon Musk is known for his ability to manage his time efficiently despite running multiple companies. He sets ambitious goals, follows strict schedules, and applies a "time blocking" technique to allocate specific time slots for different tasks and meetings.
- ✓ Marissa Mayer (Former CEO of Yahoo): Marissa Mayer implemented various time management strategies during her tenure at Yahoo. She focused on reducing meeting times, streamlining decision-making processes, and creating an environment that valued efficiency and productivity.
- ✓ Sheryl Sandberg (Facebook): Sheryl Sandberg, as the COO of Facebook, emphasizes the importance of setting priorities and managing time effectively. She promotes strategies like "don't leave before you leave" to ensure that employees maintain a healthy work-life balance and make the most of their time.

By following this action plan and drawing inspiration from successful leaders, you can develop and enhance your time management skills as a new manager. Remember to prioritize, plan, delegate, and minimize time-wasting activities to optimize your productivity, meet deadlines consistently, and maintain a healthy work-life balance.

Team Building

Understanding Team Building: Team building is the process of creating a cohesive and high-performing team. It involves developing strategies to foster collaboration, recognizing and leveraging individual strengths, promoting effective communication, and establishing a positive team culture. Managers who excel in team building can create an environment where team members work together towards shared goals and achieve outstanding results.

Benefits and Importance of Team Building:

- ✓ Enhanced Productivity: Effective team building improves team dynamics and collaboration, resulting in increased productivity. When team members work well together, they can share responsibilities, support one another, and leverage their collective skills and knowledge to achieve goals efficiently.
- ✓ Improved Problem-Solving: A strong team that collaborates well can approach problem-solving with diverse perspectives and experiences. Team building facilitates effective communication, creativity, and innovative thinking, leading to better problem-solving outcomes.
- ✓ Increased Employee Engagement: Team building activities promote a sense of belonging and engagement among team members. When employees feel valued, supported, and connected to their team, they are more likely to be motivated, satisfied, and committed to their work.

- ✓ Synergy and Innovation: Team building encourages the exchange of ideas, knowledge, and skills among team members. By fostering a culture of open communication and trust, managers can create an environment that promotes synergy and sparks innovation.
- ✓ Retention and Talent Development: Strong team dynamics and a positive team culture contribute to employee satisfaction and retention. When managers invest in team building, they enhance employee morale, create growth opportunities, and cultivate a supportive work environment that attracts and retains top talent.

Action Plan to Develop Team Building Skills:

- ✓ Set Clear Team Goals: Clearly define team goals, objectives, and expectations. Ensure that team members understand the purpose and importance of their collective efforts. Clearly communicate the team's vision and align individual goals with the team's objectives.
- ✓ Foster Effective Communication: Encourage open and transparent communication within the team. Establish channels for sharing information, ideas, and feedback. Actively listen to team members, promote respectful dialogue, and address conflicts or concerns promptly.
- ✓ Recognize Individual Strengths: Understand the strengths and capabilities of each team member. Recognize and leverage individual strengths to assign tasks and responsibilities effectively. Encourage cross-training and

knowledge sharing to enhance the overall skill set of the team.

- ✓ Promote Collaboration: Create opportunities for collaboration and teamwork. Assign projects or tasks that require cooperation and joint problem-solving. Encourage team members to share knowledge, support one another, and celebrate collective achievements.
- ✓ Cultivate a Positive Team Culture: Foster a positive and inclusive team culture. Promote respect, trust, and mutual support among team members. Encourage a healthy work-life balance and recognize and appreciate individual and team accomplishments.

Examples from the Corporate World:

- ✓ Sundar Pichai (Google): Sundar Pichai, as the CEO of Google, emphasizes the importance of team collaboration and building a supportive work environment. He encourages teams to work together on innovative projects, promoting a culture of collaboration and collective problem-solving.
- ✓ Mary Barra (General Motors): Mary Barra, the CEO of General Motors, prioritizes team building and collaboration to drive the company's success. She has focused on creating cross-functional teams, encouraging knowledge sharing, and fostering a culture of open communication and teamwork.
- ✓ Richard Branson (Virgin Group): Richard Branson, the founder of Virgin Group, emphasizes the importance of building strong teams. He believes that a positive and collaborative team culture drives business

success and encourages a supportive and inclusive work environment.

By following this action plan and drawing inspiration from successful leaders, you can develop and enhance your team building skills as a new manager. Remember to prioritize effective communication, recognize individual strengths, promote collaboration, and cultivate a positive team culture. By doing so, you can create a high-performing team that achieves exceptional results.

Strategic Thinking

Understanding Strategic Thinking: Strategic thinking is the ability to think beyond day-to-day operations and take a long-term, big-picture perspective. Managers who possess this skill can analyze complex situations, anticipate future trends, identify opportunities, and make decisions that align with their organization's long-term objectives. Strategic thinking involves considering multiple perspectives, understanding the competitive landscape, and adapting strategies to meet changing conditions.

Benefits and Importance of Strategic Thinking:

- ✓ Vision and Direction: Strategic thinking helps managers define a compelling vision and set a clear direction for their team. By understanding the broader goals and objectives of the organization, managers can align their team's efforts and make informed decisions that contribute to long-term success.
- ✓ Adaptability and Agility: Strategic thinkers can anticipate and respond effectively to changes in the business environment. By analyzing trends, market dynamics, and emerging opportunities, managers can proactively adjust strategies and seize competitive advantages.
- ✓ Effective Resource Allocation: Strategic thinking enables managers to allocate resources effectively. By understanding the organization's priorities, managers can allocate budgets, personnel, and other resources to initiatives that have the greatest impact on achieving long-term goals.

- ✓ Decision-Making: Strategic thinkers make informed decisions based on a deep understanding of the organization's goals and the implications of their choices. They consider long-term consequences, evaluate risks, and weigh alternatives to ensure decisions align with the strategic direction.
- ✓ Innovation and Growth: Strategic thinkers are catalysts for innovation and growth. By analyzing market trends, customer needs, and competitive forces, managers can identify new opportunities, develop innovative solutions, and drive the organization forward.

Action Plan to Develop Strategic Thinking Skills:

- ✓ Understand the Organization's Strategy: Gain a comprehensive understanding of your organization's mission, vision, and strategic objectives. Familiarize yourself with the broader context in which your team operates, including industry trends, competitive landscape, and key stakeholders.
- ✓ Analyze and Anticipate: Develop the ability to analyze complex situations and anticipate future trends. Stay informed about industry developments, emerging technologies, and market shifts. Seek out diverse perspectives and engage in scenario planning exercises to enhance your ability to think strategically.
- ✓ Identify Opportunities and Risks: Identify opportunities for growth and improvement within your team and the organization. Assess potential risks and consider the impact of different courses of action. Evaluate the feasibility, potential impact, and alignment with

long-term goals before pursuing new initiatives.

- ✓ Foster a Learning Culture: Encourage continuous learning and curiosity within your team. Support knowledge sharing, provide opportunities for professional development, and encourage team members to stay updated on industry trends and best practices.
- ✓ Collaborate and Seek Input: Engage with colleagues, superiors, and team members to gain different perspectives. Encourage open dialogue and collaboration to foster innovative thinking. Seek feedback on your ideas and decisions to refine your strategic thinking skills.

Examples from the Corporate World:

- ✓ Jeff Bezos (Amazon): Jeff Bezos, as the founder and former CEO of Amazon, is known for his strategic thinking. He envisioned Amazon as a customer-centric company and expanded its offerings beyond books to become a global e-commerce and cloud computing giant.
- ✓ Ginni Rometty (IBM): Ginni Rometty, the former CEO of IBM, focused on transforming the company's business strategy to adapt to the changing technology landscape. Under her leadership, IBM shifted its focus to emerging technologies such as artificial intelligence and cloud computing.
- ✓ Elon Musk (Tesla, SpaceX): Elon Musk is recognized for his strategic thinking and vision. With Tesla, he aimed to accelerate the adoption of sustainable energy by producing electric vehicles. Through SpaceX, he

envisions colonizing Mars and revolutionizing space travel.

By following this action plan and drawing inspiration from successful strategic thinkers, you can develop and enhance your strategic thinking skills as a new manager. Remember to understand the organization's strategy, analyze and anticipate trends, identify opportunities, and foster a learning culture within your team. With strategic thinking, you can guide your team towards long-term success and contribute to the achievement of organizational goals.

Influence and Persuasion

Understanding Influence and Persuasion: Influence and persuasion skills are essential for managers to gain buy-in, rally support, and drive change within their teams and organizations. Managers with strong influence and persuasion skills can effectively communicate their ideas, build relationships, negotiate, and navigate complex stakeholder dynamics. These skills allow managers to inspire and motivate others, foster collaboration, and achieve desired outcomes.

Benefits and Importance of Influence and Persuasion:

- ✓ Gaining Buy-in: Influence and persuasion skills help managers gain buy-in for their ideas and initiatives. By effectively articulating the benefits, aligning interests, and addressing concerns of stakeholders, managers can secure support and cooperation.
- ✓ Driving Change: Change initiatives often encounter resistance. Managers with strong influence and persuasion skills can overcome resistance by building trust, presenting a compelling case for change, and engaging stakeholders in the change process. This increases the likelihood of successful implementation.
- ✓ Building Strong Relationships: Influence and persuasion skills enable managers to build strong relationships with team members, peers, and senior leaders. By establishing credibility, actively listening, and understanding others' perspectives, managers

foster trust, collaboration, and a positive work environment.

- ✓ Effective Negotiation: Influential managers excel in negotiation. They can advocate for their team's needs, find mutually beneficial solutions, and handle conflicts effectively. Strong negotiation skills help managers achieve win-win outcomes, maintain relationships, and resolve differences constructively.
- ✓ Enhancing Leadership Impact: Influence and persuasion skills enhance a manager's leadership impact. Managers who can effectively influence and persuade others can inspire, motivate, and mobilize their teams to achieve high performance and exceed goals.

Action Plan to Develop Influence and Persuasion Skills:

- ✓ Understand Your Audience: Familiarize yourself with the needs, interests, and perspectives of your stakeholders. Understand their communication styles and preferences. Tailor your messages and approach to resonate with different audiences, demonstrating empathy and understanding.
- ✓ Build Relationships: Invest time and effort in building strong relationships with stakeholders. Be genuine, trustworthy, and supportive. Actively listen to their concerns, offer help, and demonstrate your commitment to their success. Building relationships creates a foundation for effective influence and persuasion.
- ✓ Enhance Communication Skills: Hone your communication skills to effectively convey

your ideas and influence others. Develop clarity in your message, use persuasive language, and articulate the benefits and impact of your proposals. Practice active listening to understand others' perspectives and respond thoughtfully.

- ✓ Develop Negotiation Skills: Develop negotiation skills to handle conflicts and reach mutually beneficial outcomes. Learn techniques such as win-win negotiation, principled negotiation, and problem-solving approaches. Practice active problem-solving and seek creative solutions that satisfy the interests of all parties involved.
- ✓ Build a Track Record of Success: Demonstrate competence and build credibility by delivering on your commitments and achieving results. Build a track record of successful projects and initiatives. Use your successes as evidence to support your proposals and increase your influence over time.

Examples from the Corporate World:

- ✓ Steve Jobs (Apple): Steve Jobs, co-founder of Apple, was known for his influential and persuasive communication style. His product launches and keynote speeches were masterful demonstrations of persuasion, inspiring customers, employees, and stakeholders alike.
- ✓ Oprah Winfrey (OWN Network): Oprah Winfrey, media mogul and founder of OWN Network, has influenced and persuaded millions through her talk shows, interviews, and philanthropic efforts. Her ability to connect

with audiences and inspire action has made her an influential figure in media.

- ✓ Mary Barra (General Motors): Mary Barra, CEO of General Motors, has demonstrated influence and persuasion skills in leading the transformation of the company. Her ability to communicate a compelling vision, gain buy-in from stakeholders, and drive cultural change has been instrumental in GM's turnaround.

By following this action plan and drawing inspiration from successful leaders, you can develop and enhance your influence and persuasion skills as a new manager. Remember to understand your audience, build relationships, enhance communication skills, develop negotiation abilities, and build a track record of success. Effective influence and persuasion skills enable you to gain buy-in, drive change, and inspire others to achieve desired outcomes.

Delegation

Understanding Delegation: Delegation is the process of assigning tasks and responsibilities to team members while empowering them to take ownership and deliver results. Effective delegation involves assessing team members' skills, providing clear instructions and resources, and trusting their abilities to accomplish the assigned tasks. As a manager, delegation allows you to focus on higher-level responsibilities and fosters professional growth within your team.

Benefits and Importance of Delegation:

- ✓ Improved Time Management: Delegating tasks allows managers to distribute workload effectively, freeing up time for strategic planning, decision-making, and higher-level responsibilities. It helps managers prioritize their time and focus on tasks that require their expertise and attention.
- ✓ Skill Development: Delegation provides team members with opportunities to develop new skills and expand their capabilities. By assigning challenging tasks and providing necessary support and feedback, managers foster professional growth and increase the overall skill set of the team.
- ✓ Empowerment and Engagement: Delegation empowers team members by entrusting them with meaningful responsibilities. This increases their sense of ownership, engagement, and job satisfaction. When employees feel trusted and valued, they are

more motivated to contribute and perform at their best.

- ✓ Enhanced Collaboration: Delegation promotes collaboration within the team. By involving team members in decision-making and task ownership, managers foster a collaborative environment where knowledge and expertise are shared. This leads to improved teamwork, communication, and the generation of innovative ideas.
- ✓ Succession Planning: Delegation prepares team members for future leadership roles and builds a pipeline of talent within the organization. By delegating responsibilities and providing developmental opportunities, managers identify potential successors and groom them for higher-level positions.

Action Plan to Develop Delegation Skills:

- ✓ Assess Team Members' Skills: Understand the skills, strengths, and capabilities of each team member. Evaluate their past performance, level of expertise, and developmental needs. This assessment helps in assigning tasks that align with their abilities and provide growth opportunities.
- ✓ Define Clear Expectations: Clearly communicate the objectives, expectations, and desired outcomes of the delegated task. Provide comprehensive instructions, guidelines, and any necessary resources. Ensure team members have a clear understanding of their responsibilities and deadlines.
- ✓ Provide Support and Guidance: Offer ongoing support and guidance to team members as

they undertake delegated tasks. Be available to answer questions, provide clarification, and offer advice when needed. Provide constructive feedback and recognize achievements to motivate and develop their skills.

- ✓ Foster a Culture of Trust: Build trust with your team members by demonstrating confidence in their abilities. Delegate tasks that match their skill level and provide them with autonomy and decision-making authority. Trusting their judgment and showing appreciation for their contributions boosts their confidence and performance.
- ✓ Review and Evaluate: Regularly review the progress and outcomes of delegated tasks. Provide feedback to team members, highlighting areas of success and areas for improvement. Use this opportunity to assess their development and identify additional growth opportunities.

Examples from the Corporate World:

- ✓ Jeff Bezos (Amazon): Jeff Bezos, as the founder and former CEO of Amazon, emphasized the importance of delegation. He delegated tasks and decision-making authority to his leadership team, allowing them to take ownership and drive innovation within their respective areas of responsibility.
- ✓ Mary Barra (General Motors): Mary Barra, the CEO of General Motors, delegates tasks to her executive team, empowering them to make decisions and drive the company's strategy. Her delegation style allows for

collaboration and promotes the development of future leaders within the organization.

- ✓ Tim Cook (Apple): Tim Cook, the CEO of Apple, is known for his effective delegation skills. He delegates various operational responsibilities, allowing him to focus on long-term strategic planning and vision. His delegation style enables Apple's teams to excel in their respective areas.

By following this action plan and drawing inspiration from successful leaders, you can develop and enhance your delegation skills as a new manager. Remember to assess skills, communicate expectations clearly, provide support and guidance, foster a culture of trust, and review progress. Effective delegation empowers your team, promotes skill development, and allows you to focus on strategic responsibilities.

Conflict Resolution

Understanding Conflict Resolution: Conflict resolution is the process of addressing and resolving conflicts within a team or organization. Managers who possess this skill can effectively manage interpersonal conflicts, disagreements, and differences of opinion. Conflict resolution involves active listening, empathy, effective communication, negotiation, and finding mutually beneficial solutions. Managers who excel in conflict resolution foster a harmonious work environment and strengthen team dynamics.

Benefits and Importance of Conflict Resolution:

- ✓ Improved Relationships: Effective conflict resolution strengthens relationships among team members. By addressing conflicts constructively, managers promote open communication, trust, and collaboration. This leads to stronger bonds and a more positive work environment.
- ✓ Increased Productivity: Resolving conflicts promptly and effectively prevents them from escalating and affecting team productivity. By addressing conflicts, managers create a more harmonious and focused work environment, allowing team members to concentrate on their tasks and goals.
- ✓ Enhanced Problem-Solving: Conflict resolution encourages diverse perspectives and creative problem-solving. By addressing conflicts constructively, managers create an environment where different viewpoints are

valued and considered, leading to innovative solutions and improved decision-making.

- ✓ Reduced Stress and Tension: Unresolved conflicts can create tension and stress within a team. Effective conflict resolution helps alleviate these negative emotions and promotes a healthier work environment. When conflicts are addressed and resolved, team members can focus on their work without the distraction of unresolved issues.
- ✓ Retention and Engagement: Conflict resolution contributes to employee retention and engagement. When conflicts are resolved in a fair and respectful manner, team members feel heard, valued, and supported. This fosters job satisfaction, improves employee morale, and increases retention rates.

Action Plan to Develop Conflict Resolution Skills:

- ✓ Develop Self-Awareness: Understand your own conflict management style, triggers, and biases. Reflect on how you typically respond to conflicts and identify areas for improvement. Being aware of your own emotions and reactions allows you to approach conflicts with greater objectivity.
- ✓ Practice Active Listening: Engage in active listening during conflicts. Pay attention to both verbal and non-verbal cues, demonstrate empathy, and seek to understand the underlying concerns and needs of all parties involved. Paraphrase and summarize to ensure you have understood the perspectives accurately.

- ✓ Foster Effective Communication: Enhance your communication skills to facilitate constructive conflict resolution. Use clear and non-confrontational language, ask open-ended questions, and encourage open dialogue. Create a safe and respectful space where team members can express their viewpoints.
- ✓ Seek Win-Win Solutions: Aim for mutually beneficial solutions that address the underlying concerns of all parties involved. Explore options, encourage brainstorming, and facilitate negotiation to find compromises and resolutions that meet the needs of everyone involved.
- ✓ Mediate and Facilitate: In more complex conflicts, act as a mediator or facilitator. Remain impartial, guide the discussion, and ensure that all voices are heard. Help identify common ground, manage emotions, and steer the conversation towards constructive problem-solving.

Examples from the Corporate World:

- ✓ Satya Nadella (Microsoft): Satya Nadella, as the CEO of Microsoft, focuses on fostering a collaborative and inclusive work culture. Under his leadership, Microsoft has implemented conflict resolution training programs and established channels for open communication to address conflicts effectively.
- ✓ Mary Barra (General Motors): Mary Barra, the CEO of General Motors, emphasizes the importance of open communication and conflict resolution within the organization. She encourages team members to engage in

constructive dialogue, address conflicts promptly, and find solutions that align with the company's goals.

- ✓ Elon Musk (Tesla, SpaceX): Elon Musk, the CEO of Tesla and SpaceX, has emphasized the need for constructive conflict resolution within his organizations. He encourages open debate, challenging ideas, and finding the best solutions through robust discussions while maintaining a respectful and collaborative environment.

By following this action plan and drawing inspiration from successful leaders, you can develop and enhance your conflict resolution skills as a new manager. Remember to develop self-awareness, practice active listening, foster effective communication, seek win-win solutions, and mediate when necessary. Effective conflict resolution strengthens relationships, improves productivity, and fosters a positive work environment.

Coaching and Mentoring

Understanding Coaching and Mentoring: Coaching and mentoring involve supporting the growth and development of individuals within your team. As a manager, you act as a coach and mentor by providing guidance, feedback, and resources to help team members reach their full potential. This involves identifying their strengths and areas for improvement, setting development goals, and offering support throughout their professional journey.

Benefits and Importance of Coaching and Mentoring:

- ✓ Employee Growth and Development: Coaching and mentoring contribute to the growth and development of team members. By providing guidance and support, managers help individuals enhance their skills, knowledge, and performance. This leads to increased job satisfaction, engagement, and professional growth.
- ✓ Improved Performance: Coaching and mentoring facilitate improved performance and productivity. By offering constructive feedback, managers help individuals identify areas for improvement and develop strategies to overcome challenges. This enhances their ability to meet goals and achieve higher levels of performance.
- ✓ Succession Planning: Coaching and mentoring contribute to succession planning by identifying high-potential individuals within the team. Managers who invest in coaching and mentoring develop future leaders,

ensuring a pipeline of talent for the organization.

- ✓ Enhanced Engagement and Retention: When managers provide coaching and mentoring, team members feel valued and supported. This fosters a sense of engagement and loyalty, leading to increased employee retention. Coaching and mentoring create a positive work environment that attracts and retains top talent.
- ✓ Knowledge Sharing and Team Collaboration: Coaching and mentoring promote knowledge sharing and collaboration within the team. By sharing expertise and offering guidance, managers facilitate a culture of learning and collaboration, where team members support and learn from each other.

Action Plan to Develop Coaching and Mentoring Skills:

- ✓ Build Rapport: Establish open and trusting relationships with team members. Take the time to understand their aspirations, strengths, and development areas. Show empathy, actively listen, and demonstrate genuine care for their growth and well-being.
- ✓ Set Clear Goals: Collaborate with team members to set clear and meaningful development goals. Align these goals with their aspirations and the needs of the organization. Ensure goals are specific, measurable, attainable, relevant, and time-bound (SMART).
- ✓ Provide Constructive Feedback: Offer regular and constructive feedback to help individuals identify areas for improvement and celebrate

their successes. Be specific, balanced, and focused on behaviors and outcomes. Provide actionable recommendations for growth and improvement.

- ✓ Offer Guidance and Resources: Provide guidance, resources, and learning opportunities to support the development of team members. Recommend relevant training programs, assign stretch projects, or provide access to industry-specific resources. Encourage continuous learning and personal development.
- ✓ Encourage Reflection and Self-Assessment: Encourage individuals to reflect on their progress, strengths, and areas for improvement. Support their self-assessment and help them identify strategies to address their development needs. Foster a growth mindset that embraces continuous improvement.

Examples from the Corporate World:

- ✓ Bill Campbell (Former CEO and Coach): Bill Campbell, known as "The Coach" in Silicon Valley, coached and mentored several top executives in companies such as Apple, Google, and Intuit. His coaching approach focused on building strong relationships, providing candid feedback, and supporting the personal and professional growth of his mentees.
- ✓ Indra Nooyi (Former CEO of PepsiCo): Indra Nooyi emphasized coaching and mentoring throughout her tenure as CEO of PepsiCo. She mentored several employees, guiding their careers and helping them reach

leadership positions within the company. Her commitment to coaching and mentoring fostered a culture of growth and development within PepsiCo.

- ✓ Eric Schmidt (Former CEO of Google): Eric Schmidt served as a mentor to Larry Page and Sergey Brin, the founders of Google. His guidance and support were instrumental in shaping Google's growth and success. Schmidt emphasized the importance of coaching and mentoring in developing future leaders.

By following this action plan and drawing inspiration from successful leaders, you can develop and enhance your coaching and mentoring skills as a new manager. Remember to build rapport, set clear goals, provide constructive feedback, offer guidance and resources, and encourage reflection and self-assessment. Effective coaching and mentoring contribute to the growth, performance, and engagement of your team members, fostering a culture of continuous learning and development.

Continuous Learning

Understanding Continuous Learning: Continuous learning is the ongoing process of acquiring new knowledge, skills, and insights to stay updated and improve performance. Successful managers understand the importance of lifelong learning and actively seek opportunities to enhance their expertise, stay abreast of industry trends, and adapt to changing business environments.

Benefits and Importance of Continuous Learning:

- ✓ Professional Growth: Continuous learning enables managers to expand their knowledge, skills, and capabilities. It enhances their professional growth and opens up new opportunities for advancement within their field or organization.
- ✓ Adaptability: Learning is essential for adapting to evolving industry trends, technologies, and best practices. Managers who engage in continuous learning are better equipped to embrace change, make informed decisions, and lead their teams through dynamic environments.
- ✓ Innovation and Creativity: Continuous learning fosters a mindset of innovation and creativity. Managers who consistently acquire new knowledge and perspectives are more likely to generate fresh ideas, identify novel solutions, and drive innovation within their teams and organizations.
- ✓ Enhanced Problem-Solving: Continuous learning equips managers with diverse tools and approaches to tackle complex challenges.

By expanding their knowledge base, they can apply critical thinking skills, draw from various disciplines, and develop effective problem-solving strategies.

- ✓ Employee Engagement: Managers who prioritize continuous learning set a positive example for their team members. By investing in their own development, they inspire and motivate employees to pursue their own learning and growth. This, in turn, enhances employee engagement and creates a culture of continuous improvement.

Action Plan to Develop Continuous Learning Skills:

- ✓ Identify Learning Goals: Reflect on your strengths and areas for improvement. Identify specific knowledge or skills you want to develop. Set measurable and achievable learning goals that align with your career aspirations and the needs of your role.
- ✓ Stay Informed: Stay updated on industry trends, best practices, and emerging technologies. Subscribe to industry publications, join professional associations, and follow thought leaders in your field. Engage in networking activities to exchange knowledge and insights with peers.
- ✓ Pursue Professional Development: Seek out professional development opportunities such as seminars, workshops, conferences, or webinars. Attend relevant training programs or certifications to deepen your expertise in specific areas. Take advantage of online learning platforms to access a wide range of courses and resources.

- ✓ Seek Feedback and Mentoring: Regularly seek feedback from your team members, superiors, and mentors. Embrace constructive criticism as an opportunity for growth. Actively seek mentors who can provide guidance, share their experiences, and challenge you to push beyond your comfort zone.
- ✓ Foster a Learning Culture: Create a culture of continuous learning within your team. Encourage knowledge sharing, organize lunch and learn sessions, or establish a mentorship program. Recognize and reward employees who prioritize learning and professional growth.

Examples from the Corporate World:

- ✓ Satya Nadella (Microsoft): Satya Nadella, the CEO of Microsoft, emphasizes the importance of continuous learning. Under his leadership, Microsoft has transformed its culture to embrace learning and growth, empowering employees to expand their skills and adapt to the evolving technology landscape.
- ✓ Sheryl Sandberg (Facebook): Sheryl Sandberg, the COO of Facebook, promotes continuous learning as a key driver of success. She encourages employees to engage in ongoing development, offers resources for learning, and supports a culture of continuous improvement.
- ✓ Warren Buffett (Berkshire Hathaway): Warren Buffett, the legendary investor and CEO of Berkshire Hathaway, is known for his commitment to continuous learning. He spends a significant amount of time reading and acquiring new knowledge to inform his

investment decisions and stay ahead in the ever-changing financial landscape.

By following this action plan and drawing inspiration from successful leaders, you can develop and enhance your continuous learning skills as a new manager. Remember to set learning goals, stay informed, pursue professional development, seek feedback, and foster a learning culture within your team. By doing so, you can continuously grow, adapt, and excel in your role as a manager.

Conclusion

Congratulations on completing this journey through the pages of this book: **'From Aspiring to Inspiring: A Guide for New Managers on the Rise'**! We hope that the insights, strategies, and examples shared have provided you with a solid foundation for success as a newly promoted manager or an aspiring one.

Becoming an effective manager is not an endpoint but rather a continuous journey of growth and development. It requires dedication, self-reflection, and a commitment to honing your skills and abilities. Remember that true leadership is not just about the title you hold, but about the impact you make and the positive influence you have on those around you.

Throughout this book, we have explored various skills and attributes essential for managerial success. From leadership and communication to decision-making and problem-solving, each chapter has provided you with actionable steps and practical examples to help you navigate the complexities of your managerial role.

However, acquiring knowledge is just the first step. The true value lies in applying what you have learned. We encourage you to take the concepts, strategies, and tools presented in this book and incorporate them into your everyday practice. Embrace challenges as opportunities for growth, seek feedback from your team and colleagues, and continuously strive to improve your skills and effectiveness as a manager.

Remember, leadership is not solely about your own achievements but also about empowering others to reach their full potential. Foster a culture of collaboration, trust, and open communication within your team. Support the growth and development of your team members, provide them with opportunities to shine, and celebrate their successes along the way.

As you embark on your managerial journey, always keep in mind the importance of self-care and work-life balance. Balancing the demands of your role with personal well-being is crucial for sustainable success. Take time to recharge, invest in your own development, and nurture your own passions and interests outside of work.

Lastly, never stop learning. The business world is constantly evolving, and as a manager, you must stay adaptable, open to new ideas, and eager to expand your knowledge. Embrace new technologies, seek out professional development opportunities, and surround yourself with mentors and colleagues who can inspire and challenge you.

We sincerely hope that this book has provided you with the insights and inspiration needed to thrive in your managerial role. Remember, you have the power to make a significant impact and create positive change within your team and organization. We believe in your potential and wish you every success in your managerial journey.

About the Author 'GERARD ASSEY'

Gerard Assey is a Graduate in Economics, a PGD in Management (HRD) and holds a Doctorate in Leadership. Gerard holds several International Qualifications in Sales, Debt Collection, Training & Teaching, and is a 'Fellow' of the prestigious 'Institute of Sales & Marketing Management'-UK, a Certified NLP Practitioner, a 'Certified Trainer', an 'Accredited Management Teacher-Behavioral Sciences', a 'Certified Competency Facilitator', a 'Certified Management Consultant'- (the International credentials of a professional management consultant, awarded in accordance with global standards of the ICMCI); and a Certification from the University of Michigan in 'Successful Negotiation: Essential Strategies and Skills'

He is also a Member of the 'National Association of Sales Professionals' backed with several years experience in varied industries, both in India and Overseas. He also holds an 'Etiquette Consultant' Certification from the USA (by Sue Fox, Author of Best Seller: 'Business Etiquette for Dummies'. She has trained some of the top celebrities' world over). He was also a recipient of a scholarship for extensive training in Japan on 'Corporate Management for India'.

Gerard Assey is 'Founder & Chief Corporate Trainer' of the Group: '**Citius, Altius, Fortius Unlimited**'- an organization that **celebrated 20 years of Glorious Service** in 2021, focusing on 3 Core Competencies:

People. Performance. Profit; in functional areas of Sales & Marketing, HR & Organizational Development, covering Recruitment, Training & Consultancy!

Having managed organizations with large Sales Forces in India & Overseas, his specialization cover extensive areas of Sales Training (All levels - Presentation, Negotiation, Key/ Strategic Accounts Management & Managerial Skills for all sectors), Bid Proposal/ Capture Planning/ Management Trainings, Retail Sales, Customer Service & Customer Retention Programs, Training for Prevention & Collection of Debt, Self & Personal Development Programs (Time Management, Teamwork & Team Building, Business Etiquette & Personal Grooming, Leadership & Managerial Skills, People Management Skills, Train-the-Trainer etc), including preparation of Custom-designed Business Manuals for Internal (HR, Induction, and Sales etc) & External use (Instruction, User Manuals).

Gerard has successfully conducted over 5980 Trainings & Workshops (as of Aug '23) all across India, Middle East, Africa, Europe & S.E. Asia. Besides public programs conducted regularly, both in India & Overseas, he has some of the top names as clients whom he services from Single Owners to large Public & Government undertakings, covering all sectors, for their in-house needs.

His website: www.CollectionSkills.com is the only one in this part of the world to be featured in the 'Collections & Credit Risk Magazine-USA' under 'Who's Who in Training' and ranks TOP, along with other websites listed below on most search engines.

Gerard is author of 75 books already (Sept 2023),

A few of the business related books being:

1. Bite-sized Bits on Commonsense Management
2. Heart to Heart on Life's Principles'
3. How to become a Successful Manager
4. The Sales Professionals' Master Workbook of S.Y.S.T.E.M.S
5. The Professional Business Email Etiquette Handbook & Guide
6. The Professional Business Video-Conferencing Etiquette Handbook & Guide
7. Professional Presentation Skills
8. Exceptional Customer Service
9. Professional Tele-Marketing Skills
10. Professional Debt Collection Skills
11. The G.R.E.A.T. Sales & Service Workbook
12. Sales Training Advantage for Results (*The Ultimate Sales Training Manual to enable you stand out as a S.T.A.R.*)
13. CEO Daily Planner & Organizer
14. The Sales Professionals' Master Daily Planner
15. The Professional Debt Collector's Master Daily Planner
16. My Daily Planner & Organizer
17. MY EMERGENCY INFORMATION RECORD (Family Emergency & Peace of Mind Planner)
18. The Ultimate Therapist & Counselors Planner and Organizer
19. Building an Ethical Workplace
20. Managing Relationships at Work
21. Managing Business Meetings Effectively
22. Effective Delegation Skills
23. Goal Setting for Success
24. B2B Selling by Email
25. Professional Business Etiquette & Grooming
26. Dining Etiquette & Table Manners
27. Effective Networking Skills
28. Grooming, Etiquette & Manners for Teens, Young Adults & Future Leaders
29. Inter-Personal Skills
30. Get Ready, Get Hired!
31. Selling in a Recession
32. Effective Receivables Management in an Economic Downturn!
33. Real Estate & Property Sales Training

34. Credit Sales & Accounts Receivable Management
35. Selling Skills for Real Estate & Property Advisors
36. Take G.R.E.A.T. C.A.R.E!
37. Spa, Salon & Health Club Selling Skills
38. Selling Travel, Holiday & MICE Services
39. Selling Skills for Spa's, Salons & Health Clubs
40. Retailing in Salons & Spas
41. Selling Holiday, Vacation, Tours & Packages
42. The Power of Sales Referrals
43. Selling Luxury
44. Technical Selling Skills Financial Advisors Sales Training
45. Dealing with Burnout at Work
46. Monopolize Your Markets
47. Selling to Affluent Customers
48. Financial Selling Skills
49. The Effective Manager's Guide: Key Skills to Thrive
50. From Aspiring to Inspiring: A Guide for New Managers on the Rise

Besides regularly contributing to business & trade journals, including international ones such as the 'Creative Training Techniques' and the 'Sales News' of the U.S.A, He is also a member of several prestigious bodies & trade associations, having participated in many Conferences & Workshops in India & Overseas.
Prior to his last assignment of leading & managing a large MNC as head, Gerard had a 3-year stint in the Middle East as a Consultant with a leading British Consultancy Firm.

As the past 'Official Country Representative' for the International Business Award- 'THE STEVIES'-(the business world's own Oscar) for about 4 years- he ensured a few Indian companies that qualify for the same every year!

Gerard can be contacted at:
Email: training@Sales-Training.in,training@CollectionSkills.com
Websites:
www.Sales-Training.in
www.EtiquetteWorks.in
www.CollectionSkills.com
www.RetailSalesTraining.in
www.SalesTrainingIndia.com
www.ManualPreparation.com
www.TrainingWithPuppets.com
www.FirstContactAcademy.com
www.SalesAndMarketingRecruiter.com

Our TRAININGS & BOOKS that can help your team

- ✓ **Sales Effectiveness**: Selling Skills for any Sector: Service/ Logistics/ FMCG Realty/ Insurance & Finance/ Media/ SPA's, Health Clubs & Salons/ Key Account Management, Effective Negotiation Skills/ Bid & Proposal Management Skills/ Retail Sales Training: Any Sector (Auto, Jewelry, Clothing, Luxury etc)
- ✓ **Customer Service Skills**-Complaints Handling & Customer Retention
- ✓ **Debt Prevention & Collection Skills**
- ✓ **Etiquette & Grooming**
- ✓ **Leadership & Managerial Skills**
- ✓ **Self & Personal Development Skills**: Presentation Skills/ Effective Communication Skills/Business Proposal Writing Skills/ Problem Solving & Decision Making Skills/ Empowering Secretaries-The perfect PA! (For Secretaries & PA's)/ Effective Time Management/ Teamwork & Teambuilding/ P.R.I.D.E- **P**ersonal **R**esponsibility **I**n **D**elivering **E**xcellence

A Few of Our Business Books
By the Top Corporate Trainer & Author of 75 Books! (Sep '23)
And...DAILY PLANNERS for Every Corporate Need!
All Books available Online on all leading Stores in E-book & Paperback Formats
Experts in Training for over 22 years:
Sales, Debt Prevention & Collection, Etiquette & Grooming,
Leadership & Managerial Skills, Self & Personal Development Programs
By the Top Corporate Trainer
& Author of 75 Published Books (Sep'23)

www.ingramcontent.com/pod-product-compliance
Lightning Source LLC
LaVergne TN
LVHW010456160826
845677LV00012B/2511